Higher Modern Studies in the UK (Social Inequality)

Hannah Young

Higher Modern Studies Social Issues in the UK (Social Inequality)

What is this book about?

This book is about social inequalities in the United Kingdom.

These notes directly support the SQA Higher Modern Studies unit 'Social Issues in the United Kingdom' (Social Inequality option).

The notes assess, in detail, the following topics:

- Causes of income/wealth inequalities

- Causes of health inequalities

- The impact of inequalities on women

- The impact of inequalities on Black, Asian, and Minority Ethnic (BAME) groups

- The individualist-collectivist debate

- The effectiveness of government responses to tackling social inequalities.

How can this book help you?

•These course notes offer relevant and up-to date statistical evidence and other knowledge points from newspapers, pressure groups, government reports, think tanks, etc. The evidence is then commented upon – this is the analysis and is shown in *italics*.

•At the end of each section there is a comprehensive evaluation of the notes.

The causes of income/wealth inequality

Cause 1: Low pay/benefits

One cause of income/wealth inequality in the UK is the fact that the National Minimum Wage (NMW) is not sufficient to ensure a good standard of living. The NMW is the UK's pay floor designed to protect as many low paid workers as possible from falling into the poverty trap. In 2014 it was reported that there were 1.4 million minimum wage jobs in the UK and 5.3% are paid below or within 5p of the minimum wage. Despite the fact that in February 2015 the UK Government raised the NMW from £6.50 to £6.70 per hour for adults over the age of 21, *critics would argue that this is not enough for someone to live on and can result in income/wealth inequality as people struggle to meet their basic needs. This can also lead to an inability to save money and could result in people turning to payday loans, some of which charge up to 6000% interest. This in turn can result in a vicious cycle of poverty from which it can be difficult to escape.* In May 2017 there were approximately 6.8 million working age people in the UK claiming benefits. One of these benefits, Universal Credit (UC), was introduced in 2013 and replaced six means-tested benefits and tax credits. In 2015 the UK Government made significant cuts to the value of UC by reducing working income allowance among other financial allowances. *Critics have argued that instead of incentivising work and helping those most in need, UC has actually exacerbated income inequality.* Furthermore UC claimants have to wait at least 6 weeks between making and claim and receiving money. Citizens Advice research argued that 450,000 disabled people and their families would be worse off under universal credit. The campaign group Women's Aid have argued that as Universal Credit benefits are paid as a single payment to the household, this could have negative consequences for victims of domestic abuse. *This can cause income inequality as it disempowers women, preventing them from being financially independent. It would be fair to assess UC as having caused significant income inequality and acute financial difficulties for many who may have to turn to short term loans or even crime to feed themselves and their families. Thousands of claimants get themselves into debt, fall behind in their rent payments and face eviction while waiting for their claim to be processed. Not only does this cause income inequality it can cause homelessness.*

Cause 2: Employment

In recent years there has been a spike in the number of people employed on zero-hours contracts. It has been estimated that roughly 4% of the UK's working population – the equivalent of 1 million workers are employed on this basis. *This can cause income/wealth inequality because without guaranteed working hours and oftentimes low pay many workers will struggle to plan financially and they may also be unable to get a mortgage which can cause wealth inequality as property is an asset that can generate wealth when sold.* These contracts also lack the most fundamental of employee benefits such as sick pay. This can cause income inequality because it means that if a worker falls ill he/she may face poverty because they are not earning. Workers on zero hours contracts not only experience lack of a steady income but also no pension or redundancy payments. *This only serves to exacerbate income inequality because these workers are unable to plan financially for old age or receive compensation if their role is no longer required by the company that they are working for.*

Cause 3: Geographical location

Geography can have a significant impact in causing income/wealth inequality. Glasgow remains the most deprived city and local authority area in Scotland. Almost half (47.3%) of Glasgow's residents - 283,000 people - reside in the 20% of most deprived areas in Scotland. 34% of all children in the city were estimated to be living in poverty in 2016. In 2014, 20% of children lived in workless households, 6.5% higher than the Scottish average. *This is significant because there are more children facing a life of poverty in one area of Scotland and this is due to a low household income or workless households. Once a family becomes trapped in a persistent cycle of poverty they can spend generations on low income, without savings and facing other related social inequalities such as poor health and a lack of success in education.*

Cause 4: Lack of success in education

Lack of success in education can be a major cause of income/wealth inequality. 13% of NMW jobs are held by those with no qualifications. It has been estimated that over a course of a lifetime, a graduate from a Russell Group university will earn on average £371,000 more than someone who left school with fewer than five good GCSEs. According to Teach First the link between low income and low academic attainment is greater in the UK than almost any other developed nation. Children eligible for free school meals are less likely to get good GCSEs and go on to higher education. *This is significant because it means that some groups are more likely to struggle throughout their lives, widening social inequality. Therefore a lack of success in education is a clear driver of income/wealth inequality in the UK because without the opportunities that a good education offers some people will not be able to have a fair chance to earn a decent salary, save into a pension and get a mortgage to buy their own home.*

Evaluation

Overall, it could be argued that there are many causes of income and wealth inequality. The fact that more children are growing up in relative poverty in the UK today, particularly in Scotland, means that they will face devastating long term consequences throughout their lives. This income/wealth inequality can become so entrenched that it is almost impossible to get out of. This is because these children can become disadvantaged in terms of education and skills which will in turn limit their employment opportunities and potential to earn a good income. These children may then go on to have their own families who will have a similar experience of poverty. This is generational poverty. This shows that unemployment and/or low incomes cause a persistent poverty trap that means that some people can just meet their basic needs of food and energy, or perhaps not even these. Poorer families can experience the cycle of poverty for at least three generations and this can have a knock on effect in terms of poorer health and shorter life spans. Low pay and zero hours contracts can result in a very vulnerable financial situation for many families who face uncertainty which can lead to chaos and poor mental health. Some critics have criticised the NLW as it does not match the cost of living and almost six million people still earn less than the living wage. All of these factors are major contributors to income and wealth inequalities in the UK.

The causes of health inequality

Cause 1: Geography

Glasgow's mortality rates are the highest in Europe with life expectancy the lowest in the UK – One in four men in Glasgow die before they are 65. This is called the 'Glasgow effect'. It relates to the idea that poor health in Glasgow may be as a result of a high level of derelict land, poor social housing, vitamin D deficiency and cold winters. It has also been suggested that high levels of chromium on contaminated land where steel production took place in South Lanarkshire could be linked to cases of leukaemia and lung cancer. Lung cancer is the most common cancer in Scotland (although this may also be linked to the lifestyle choice of smoking). In 2016 the British Lung Foundation (BLF) found that people living in Glasgow were almost twice as likely to die from lung disease as those in Stirling. *Therefore it could be argued that an important cause of health inequalities in areas such as Glasgow is the history of heavy industry.* Scotland has higher rates of less common lung conditions like pneumoconiosis, caused by inhaling dusts and chemicals in the workplace. Parts of Scotland with a history of shipbuilding have high rates of the asbestos related cancer, mesothelioma *which can clearly cause health inequalities especially when these rates are compared to other shipbuilding regions of the UK such as* Tyneside where while asbestos deaths are high, they are not as high as those in West Dunbartonshire, the heart of shipbuilding in the UK particularly at the height of industrialisation and in preparation for both the First and Second World Wars.

Cause 2: Low income

Research shows that income inequality caused by low pay, unemployment and a life on benefits can cause health inequalities. In countries with unequal distributions of wealth we can see higher levels of health inequalities. According to the Equality Trust compared to other developed counties the UK has a very unequal distribution of income. The Joseph Rowntree Foundation (JRF) reported that there is a 'social gradient' in health which reveals that every step up the socio-economic ladder leads to an increase in health. *This means that those that do not have high earnings or the ability to earn will experience comparatively poorer health. This shows that there is a direct correlation between poor health and low income.* The JRF also found that the link can also be explained by 'status anxiety'. *This means that income inequality can cause stress which leads to poor health.* People who experience chronic stress are far more likely to take up smoking, drink alcohol, abuse drugs or suffer from eating disorders. All these behaviours contribute to the development of heart disease and therefore a higher mortality rate. *Therefore it would be fair to argue that while health inequalities cannot be caused by income inequalities alone, low income clearly has the potential to have a major negative impact on mental and physical health.*

Cause 3: Lifestyle choices

Lifestyle choices are the behaviours that we choose to adopt such as smoking, exercise or lack of exercise, a poor or healthy diet, drugs and alcohol. These all play a significant role in our health outcomes. Poor lifestyle choices can result in preventable chronic diseases. For example, a lack of exercise and poor diet can result in obesity and Type 2 diabetes. The NHS reported in 2018 that obesity rates are higher now than in 1995, and Scotland has some of the highest incidences of obesity for men and women among OECD countries. It concluded that lower socio-economic status is associated with higher levels of obesity. The risk of obesity in children is lowest for those living in more affluent areas. It has also been found that poor health and obesity in childhood can lead to poor health in adulthood. Childhood obesity doesn't just affect physical health. Children and teens who are overweight or obese can become depressed and have poor self-image and self-esteem. Diabetes can lead to eye disease, nerve damage, and kidney dysfunction. These examples are largely preventable by making more positive lifestyle choices. However, it could be the case that the relatively low cost of convenience foods such as McDonald's meals, the increase in the weight of snacks and propensity of 'multibuy' products such as crisps and biscuits have all led to those on low incomes purchasing these items and resulting in poor health. It may also be the case that children today live more sedentary lifestyles with hours spent in front of computer screens or smart phones. This lack of exercise coupled with a poor diet will only lead to poor health. A 2012 Cambridge University study found that healthy foods cost three times as much as unhealthy foods. Given that those on low incomes have very little money to live on, there may not be a real choice between healthy and unhealthy foods. *Therefore while poor health can be caused by poor lifestyle choices and can be experienced by all income groups and social classes, it can also be caused by low income which removes the option of choosing healthy foods that ensure good nutrition and health.* Without a good source of vitamins and minerals children will struggle to concentrate at school and this can lead to a lag in mental and physical development. *This will result in a lack of success in education which in turn will create further inequalities as they may struggle to gain qualifications, employment and a good income.*

Cause 4: Ethnicity

Ethnicity has a role to play in causing health inequalities. Some ethnicities are more susceptible to certain diseases than others. Large-scale surveys like the Health Survey for England show that BAME (Black, Asian and minority ethnic) groups as a whole are more likely to report ill-health, and that ill-health among BAME groups start at a younger age than in non-ethnic communities. Diabetes is a particular problem for Pakistanis and Bangladeshis who are over five times more likely to suffer from it than the general population. Indians of both genders are three times more at risk than any other group. According to the Mental Health

Foundation, people from BAME groups living in the UK are more likely to be diagnosed with mental health problems, more likely to be diagnosed and admitted to hospital, more likely to experience a poor outcome from treatment and more likely to disengage from mainstream mental health services, leading to social exclusion and a deterioration in their mental health. *This is important it shows a clear link between ethnicity and poor health outcomes.* It could be the case that the causes of health inequalities for BAME groups include both poverty and racism. They may also be because mainstream mental health services often fail to understand or provide services that are acceptable and accessible to non-white British communities and meet their particular cultural and other needs. *This is significa*

nt because the quality of life of BAME groups may be reduced because they may use health services less, with serious consequences for their health. This perpetuates their disproportionate levels and experience of health inequalities.

Evaluation

It is fair to evaluate that health inequalities are caused by multiple factors: culture and ethnicity, environment and lifestyle choices, to name but a few. The link between health and income inequalities is perhaps the most significant. People on low incomes tend to experience poorer health and lower life expectancy. This is certainly the case in Glasgow. It is the case that health inequalities are the most difficult of all inequalities to overcome. Poor health is a barrier to employment and therefore income, a good quality of life and stable mental health. Poor health is not an inevitability and can be caused by poor lifestyle choices, such as poor diet and a lack of exercise. That said, those on low incomes may struggle to afford a healthier diet. Furthermore, those with low incomes or those in receipt of benefits may experience social, emotional and cognitive impairment, disease, disability, and poor mental health. Poor quality housing and other environmental issues such as pollution and natural vitamin deficiencies can also cause significant health inequalities and are all linked to low income.

The impact of social inequality on women

Impact 1: Low income

Women in the UK can face low levels of income relative to their male counterparts. This is closely linked to social inequality given the lack of spending power and opportunities to invest in pensions, property and shares that are available to women as a result. Women are more likely than men to be employed in low paid jobs than men. This may be partly due to the fact that women tend to take on roles as carers for the young, sick or elderly. The Census of 2011 reported that of the 6.5 million unpaid carers in the UK 58% - 3.34 million - are women. Stepping out of work to act as a carer can prevent women from developing careers and result in income and wealth inequality. They may also have to try to find part-time employment or low paid work that has suitable hours that fits around their caring responsibilities. In 2018 the UK Government provides £64.60 per week for carers caring for someone for at least 35 hours per week. 35 hour per week constitutes the majority of the working week and works out as less than the National Minimum Wage as it equates to £1.85 per hour. *This means that women who are carers are unlikely to be able to meet their basic needs and will suffer from income and wealth inequality. They are also likely to experience a cycle of poverty on a low income.* This amount is less than an individual might live on in a developing country and as such shows that a woman in the UK on such a low income generated through the benefit of a Carer's Allowance might actually be facing absolute poverty as they are unlikely to be able to buy food, clothing and pay for rent.

Women are more likely to enter low paid sectors of the economy such as catering and cleaning, for example. According to the Low Pay Commission, approximately 70% of people in national minimum wage jobs are women. Hospitality, retail and cleaning account for 52% of NMW jobs. 59% of NMW jobs are held by women. Women also suffer from greater income/wealth inequality than men because they are more likely to be employed on a part-time or zero hour contract basis. Women account for 54% of the 1.4 million workers on temporary contracts making them more vulnerable to unemployment. 59% of those with no earnings and 67% of those with earnings below the current personal allowance are women, so will not benefit from the increase in personal income tax allowance. *The impact of this is that it can make it difficult to make financial plans, save money to purchase a house or even pay for basic necessities. It may also result in an inability to pay for childcare costs which means that some women may resort to claiming benefits such as Universal Credit rather than looking for work that fits in with childcare arrangements and pays enough to meet nursery fees.* Depending on location, the average cost of yearly full-time day nursery care for a child under two now stands at £5103 and is rising at a rate above inflation A mother over 25 being paid the NLW on a full time basis would struggle to pay for these fees, food, travel, rent etc. and so may not seek employment which would then cause income/wealth inequality. A 2011 Netmum's survey of over 2,000 working mums found that over half said they will be forced to stop work or significantly reduce their working hours as a result of the need to care for their children. A 2011 report in The Daily Mirror found that one in four mothers had to give up work because of the rising costs of childcare. *This is significant as it shows how women are impacted negatively by low income. Careers may ever begin or will be lost because of the burden of expensive childcare costs. This means that women will not be able to save, contribute to pensions or have the same disposable income as their male counterparts.*

The existence of the gender pay gap makes it difficult to recruit women to senior positions when they know they will be paid less than their male counterparts for the same role. This supports The Daily Mail's view that "The economy is losing billions of pounds because of gender segregation," compounded by the dishonourable fact that "high-flying women in Britain are paid nearly 10% less than men doing exactly the same job." Women still do not hold key positions of power in the job sector. The Equality and Human Rights Commission (EHRC) found that more than 5,400 women are missing from Britain's 26,000 most powerful posts. *The implications of the pay gap on society are numerous and do not only affect women. Gender discrimination at work constrains economic growth, increases poverty and has a negative effect on the wealth and well-being of families and communities.*

Certain groups of women are more adversely affected than others when it comes to income inequality. Almost 2.1 million pensioners living in poverty are women while 40% of ethnic minority women live in poverty, twice the proportion of white women. *Cuts to housing benefits will have a disproportionate effect on women given that 46% of housing benefit claimants are single women, compared to 20% of couples and 33% of men. Therefore it can be said that the impact of low income can be more detrimental to some women than others. In fact the most vulnerable women in UK society are most impacted by low income which means that their financial, housing and health circumstances may become increasingly worse.*

Impact 3: Lack of success in education

It could be stated that education is one area in which women face the least social inequalities. In 2010-11, there were more female (55%) than male full time undergraduates (45%) enrolled at university – a trend which shows no sign of shrinking. The latest statistics released by UCAS revealed a 22,000 drop in the number of male students enrolling at university. *This meant that last autumn women were a third more likely to start a degree than their male counterparts, despite the fact that there are actually more young men than women in the UK.* Researchers say the under-representation of male university students is down to attainment patterns in schools: girls outperform boys and are more likely to stay on at sixth form. *This is highly significant as this suggests that social inequalities in relation to education affect women far less than other factors, most notably income and employment.* That said, The Independent reported in 2014 that women were far less likely to become professors than men, only accounting for one in five of such posts. Those who do make it to the level of professorship face further discrimination – being paid on average

13.5% less than their male counterparts. *Therefore, while women do experience inequality in relation to postgraduate study, in the preceding years of their academic lives they do not experience similar discrimination.*

However, cuts to funding for mature students will affect women disproportionately as 56% of learners aged 25 and over are women. 53% of students will no longer be eligible for free ESOL (English Speakers of Other Languages) learning, of which 74% will be women. The London Economics Consultancy has estimated that with the new rates of university tuition fees, 70-80% of women students will not be able to pay off their student loans in the thirty years after they graduate. *This is significant because it shows the long-term impact of a potential lack of success in education for women in terms of income/wealth inequality, debt creation and access to education.*

Impact 2: Poor health

There is a clear link between gender and health. Despite the fact that British women live longer than men, they suffer more health problems in their lifetime. Figures in the General Household Survey suggest that women in the lowest social class group report more than twice the rate of illness of women in the highest group. Women's traditional domestic responsibilities lead them to suffer higher levels of anxiety and depression compared to males, particularly if they are on low incomes/benefits and lone parents. Analysis in 2013 by The Equality Trust has found that in the last 20 years alone, the gap in life expectancy has increased 41% for men and a staggering 73% for women. The reasons for widening health inequalities may be complex, but one contributing factor is the huge growth in economic inequality in the UK over the past 30 years. *This is of critical importance because while targeted policies and programmes have enabled women to lead healthier lives, significant gender-based health disparities remain in the UK. There is a well-established social gradient in life expectancy and health, with poorer people experiencing worse health than the wealthy.* Research suggests that this is because socio-economic inequality is itself a root or 'fundamental cause' of health inequalities. *In short, due to the unequal distribution of income, wealth and power, the wealthy are able to protect and improve their health; the poor are not.*

Women tend to have a higher rate of chronic problems such as arthritis, mental disorders, neck pain, headaches and back pain. Researchers claim that the reason for this is a mixture or biological and social factors. *This is significant because the impact of such chronic poor health is an inability to work and earn an independent income.* A person with long term ill health or physical or mental disability may have to claim Personal Independence Payment (PIP) to gain financial support. Claimants can currently receive between £21.80 and £139.75 a week, paid every four weeks, and are assessed on a points based system that takes into account their ability to carry out everyday tasks. The changes will see certain activities, such as the ability to get dressed or use the bathroom unaided, technically re-evaluated so that they now will only accrue one point as opposed to two. It is thought that the move will see 640,000 losing some, or in a minority of cases all, of their PIP support. *Considering that the majority of PIP claimants are women, it could be argued that they are disproportionately affected by the cuts, and even if reassessed and granted PIP, the amount may not be sufficient, resulting in greater income/wealth inequality. This is because PIP claimants may seek out high interest loans to simply survive. This could lead to a cycle of poverty.* The Hardest Hit, a coalition of 50 charities and organisations campaigning about the benefits system, claim that by October 2018 if the Westminster Government continued with DLA, 2.182 million disabled people of working age would be receiving some help. With PIP the number is 1.575 million – a reduction of about 608,000, the majority of which are women and *therefore they are the group most impacted by poor health and income inequalities.*

A 2012 report by the Women's Resource Centre found that carers, 58% of whom are women, are more likely to suffer from physical and mental health problems. An increase in women's unemployment and poverty, could exacerbate existing health inequality between men and women. Cuts in mental health services may particularly impact on women, who are between one and a half and two times more likely than men to suffer from anxiety and depression. *This is significant because as cuts are made to the NHS it will be women who are disproportionally affected and will experience, long term debilitating mental health issues which will impact the quality of their life and ability to work and gain an income.*

Impact 4: Employment

A significant area of social inequality facing women today relates to employment. There is a clear link between relatively poor opportunities for women to progress as far as men in their chosen careers. According to the Professional Boards Forum, women make up a very small percentage (17.3%) of FTSE board directors. Similarly, the Equality and Human Rights Commission (2011) estimates it will take 70 years at the current rate of progress to see an equal number of female and male directors of FTSE 100 companies. *This is significant because gender equality in essence promotes the equitable advancement of both men and women. This is important because this could lead to a lack of gender equality in employment in the UK, which would have a detrimental effect on women's later years, especially considering that pensions that are linked to earnings will likely be lower, resulting in elderly women living in relative poverty. The impact of low levels of gender equality in employment is that artificially reduces the pool of talent from which employers can draw upon, thereby reducing the average ability of the workforce. For women themselves, the impact could be far-reaching: it could result in low self-esteem and a perception that they are less valued in society than men.*

In March 2012, the Fawcett Society found that the unemployment rate for men stood almost exactly where it did at the end of the recession in 2009 at 1.54 million, an increase of only 0.32%, whereas female unemployment has increased by almost 20% to 1.13 million - the highest figure for 25 years. *This is significant as it shows clearly that female unemployment has grown and women experience a disproportionate level of unemployment when compared with the experience of their male counterparts.* The

Fawcett Society also found that 40% of redundancies in the last quarter were among women, up from just over 30% from the previous quarter. It is estimated that of the 500,000 public sector workers that are expected to be made unemployed due to the spending cuts, 325,000 will be women. *This is important as it reveals that even when women are in employment their positions are disproportionally more vulnerable than those of men because of the types of organisations that women tend to work for.* Ethnic minority women are more likely to be unemployed than ethnic minority men and white women – 52.8% of ethnic minority women are unemployed. Poverty.org have reported that 30% of disabled lone mothers are in employment, compared to 65% of non-disabled lone mothers. *This shows that female minority groups are more vulnerable to unemployment and therefore income/wealth inequalities. This is a negative impact as it can fuel these groups' feelings of isolation and powerlessness in society.*

Evaluation

Overall, one could argue that social inequalities have a significant impact on women in the UK particularly in relation to income and employment. Women suffer least social inequality in relation to education as they benefit from access to education at all levels and often higher grades in comparison to their male counterparts. However, some categories of women such as those from BAME communities, those with disabilities and lone parents suffer a disproportionate degree of social inequality in most areas. All things considered, when we examine the relative income levels and employment opportunities facing women today in the UK, we could feasibly conclude that women face significant social inequalities with some female minority groups experiencing more inequalities than others.

The impact of social inequality on Black, Asian and Minority Ethnic (BAME) Groups.

Impact 1: Low income

Black, Asian and Minority Ethnic (BAME) groups make up 8% of the total UK population. Throughout the UK, people from BAME groups are much more likely to be living in poverty (i.e. an income of less than 60% of the median household income) than white British people. In 2015, Pakistani and Bangladeshi communities were the most likely to be in 'persistent poverty', followed by Black African and Black Caribbean communities. *This is significant because these groups experiencing persistent poverty can be impacted negatively as they may have to turn to benefits and may even experience poor mental health as they struggle to free themselves from potentially stressful generational poverty.* In 2013/14, just under 20% of white people had 'relatively low income' after housing costs (defined as receiving less than 60% of the median average). The Black/African/Caribbean/Black British groups and 'Other' ethnic groups had just over 40% with relative low income. *This shows that some ethnic minority groups are twice as likely to experience low income as their white counterparts and this can lead to a racial-income divide in society.*

One measure of poverty relates to the eligibility of free school meals. In 2012/13, the ethnic groups most likely to be eligible were Bangladeshis (38.5%), Gypsy/Romas (47.8%) and Travellers of Irish Heritage (62%). *This is important as it shows that BAME groups are more likely than their white counterparts to be claiming income support, Jobseeker's Allowance or Universal Credit in order to receive free school meals.*

Research carried out by The Fawcett Society in 2017 found that the gender pay gap in Britain is shaped by racial inequality. Women from almost every minority ethnic group experience a pay gap with White British men. *This is significant because it shows that within some BAME groups one gender is more impacted by low income than another.* 6% of White British women are doing unpaid care work in the home, 30% and 31% of the entire populations of Pakistani and Bangladeshi women in Britain are carers. *This shows that due to the higher number of carers in these two BAME groups they are more likely to experience low income than their white counterparts. This can have a significant impact on BAME groups as they can experience less economic freedom and financial independence. BAME families may experience more debt as a result of financial instability. This can lead to less social mobility and status anxiety. BAME groups may experience higher levels of stress, low levels of happiness, increased risk of depression and higher mortality rates.* BAME groups are also much less likely to participate in social and community activities than their white counterparts because of feelings and experiences of social inequality.

Due to higher rates of worklessness and low pay in Bangladeshi households and a higher rate of lone parenthood among Black Caribbean and Black African households it is clear that some BAME groups experience more income inequalities than other groups. The Fawcett Society found that there were marked low levels of income for both Pakistani and Bangladeshi women and men. Men from these groups are by far the most likely to be working part-time, with 27% of Pakistani men and 37% of Bangladeshi men working part-time, compared to 11% of White British men. Part-time work is still predominately low paid, and one in four low paid men worked part-time in 2017. *This is significant because if the main breadwinner is only working part time hours they may experience a chaotic family life as it may be difficult to plan ahead financially and save money due to a low income. It may also lead to a reliance on credit cards and payday loans resulting in a cycle of debt and ultimately poverty.*

That said, 11% of Indian women are in top professions like medicine and law, compared to 6% of White British women. Additionally, 58% of economically active Indian women are in full-time work, compared to 51% of White British women. *This shows that while some BAME experience low income, others do not. This is important to consider as BAME are not a homogenous group. BAME are diverse in terms of income, health, employment and education inequalities and as such should not be generalised as all experiencing the same inequalities.*

Throughout the UK, BAME communities are less likely than white people to be paid the living wage. The Joseph Rowntree Foundation showed in 2015 that the ethnic group least likely to be paid below the minimum wage was white males (15.7%); and the group that which was most likely was Bangladeshi males (57.2%). *This is important as it shows that some BAME groups face low income which will negatively impact their ability to save money, purchase a home of their own and contribute to a pension to plan for old age. This means that some BAME groups will face long term income inequalities because these groups are four times more likely to earn the National Minimum Wage.*

Impact 2: Poor health

Some BAME groups are more susceptible to certain diseases than others. Levels of infant mortality are also affected by ethnicity. Cultural differences such as smoking and alcohol consumption have an impact and social issues such as poverty, harassment and discrimination also generate differences in standards of health. Large-scale surveys like the Health Survey for England show that BAME groups as a whole are more likely to report ill-health, and that ill-health among BAME groups starts at a younger age than it does in their white counterparts. Diabetes is a particular problem for Pakistanis and Bangladeshis who are over five times more likely to suffer from this lifelong condition than the general population. Indians of both genders are three times more at risk. *Therefore, poor health has a significant impact on some ethnic groups because it may result in this group being unable to participate fully in the social and economic mainstream of society. This is significant because this may manifest itself in being unable to work due to high blood pressure, the threat or impact of strokes, eye conditions, numbing in the hands and feet and kidney damage. These symptoms can have a significant impact on the quality of someone's life.* The cultural and social barriers faced by ethnic groups can mean they use health services less, with serious consequences for their health. *This perpetuates their disproportionate levels of poverty.*

A UK Government report found that BAME groups tend to have higher rates of cardiovascular disease than White people, but lower rates of cancer. Caribbean men are 50% more likely to die of stroke than the general population, but they have much lower mortality to coronary heart disease. *This is significant as it shows that some illnesses can have a negative impact on some BAME groups which can result in a lower life expectancy. This in itself has wide ranging consequences as the illnesses experienced by some BAME groups can be life-limiting and result in an inability to work and therefore an inability to earn money to support themselves and their families. The death of a breadwinner in a family can result in the remaining family members facing a life of poverty.*

A 2016 report by the Institute for Social and Economic Research at the University of Essex found that there was a 23% gap in hourly pay between black and white university graduates. Black people with A-levels were paid 14% less on average than white workers with equivalent qualifications, while those with GCSEs faced a deficit of 11%. In addition, the research showed that individuals from all ethnic minority backgrounds faced a 10% pay deficit at degree level, rising to 17% for those with A-levels alone. *This is significant as it shows that BAME are negatively impacted by low income and as a result face persistent economic disadvantages over their life time due to their ethnicity.*

Impact 3: Lack of success in education

Recent research has shown that overall, gaps in education achievement by ethnic group have narrowed considerably over the last 20 years. A 2012 report compiled by the Higher Education Academy (HEA) found that in general, more BAME females participate in Higher Education (HE) than BAME males and Black Caribbean and Bangladeshi participation rates are half those of Black African and Indian participation rates. 91% of Chinese entrants are likely to continue on to HE compared to 90% of White students and only 88.7% of Black entrants. *This shows that some*

BAME groups are marginally more likely to progress on to Higher Education which will have a positive impact on these groups as they will have more opportunities to gain qualifications on a par (or better) with their White counterparts. This will ensure a more equal society in terms of education attainment, employment opportunities and ability to earn a high salary.

The report also found that even after considering factors (prior attainment, subject of study, age, gender, disability, deprivation, type of HE institution attended, term-time accommodation and ethnicity), being from a minority ethnic group was still found to have a significant negative effect on degree attainment. *This shows that BAME groups can experience education inequality and this will result in income inequality in the long term. It also means that if BAME groups continue to experience education and income inequality, wealthier non-BAME groups will have greater economic control as wealth will be unevenly distributed among Whites which will create a fragmented society divided by ethnicity and wealth.*

According to the Institute of Student Employers (ISE) in 2011 there were over 80 graduates applying for every graduate job, and almost three-quarters of large graduate employers now routinely demand that applicants have a minimum of an upper second class degree in order to sift out applications. *This is significant as it shows that BAME groups tend to attain lower classification degrees than their white counterparts and as such they experience an attainment gap which will have an impact on their employment opportunities and ability to earn a high salary.*

Data on attainment by ethnicity was been published by the National Pupil Database in 2013. The research showed substantial improvements for Bangladeshi pupils, who on average performed less well than White British pupils in 2004, but were above average for White British pupils in 2013. *This shows an upward trend in educational achievement for this BAME group which is a positive impact.* The proportion of White 16-year-olds who do not continue in full time education is much higher than that for any other ethnic minority, but many are undertaking some form of training. In addition, 19% of all White British boys eligible for free school meals do not obtain 5 or more GCSEs. *This is significant as it shows that it is in fact White males that experience more education inequality and therefore BAME are not, in general, as negatively impacted as Whites.* Ethnic minorities experience higher GCSE attainment levels than Whites and, as such, education could be considered as an area of positivity and success. 23% of all Black African women are students, the second highest of any group of women, suggesting grounds for optimism for the longer term prospects of Black African women and a long term positive impact on employment opportunities and ability to earn a good and stable salary.

Impact 4: Employment

The Race Disparity Audit's Ethnicity Facts and Figures website, a government resource about the employment, education, housing and standard of living faced by different ethnic communities living in the UK, has shown that in 2016 unemployment among BAME groups is almost double that of White British adults. The data also found that the group with the highest rate of unemployment was Pakistani/Bangladeshi (11%), and the groups with the lowest rate were White British and White other (4%). The unemployment gap between BAME and White Britons is also greater in the north of the country, according to the data, with a 13.6% disparity reported in the north compared to 9% in the south. *This is important as it shows that in general BAME groups are negatively impacted by employment inequalities and this can be exacerbated by geographical location.* Some groups are affected by local economic circumstances because they are concentrated in areas of high unemployment. For example, the Pakistani community, which is concentrated in the North and Midlands of England, was negatively affected by the closure of manufacturing industries in these areas.

According to the 'Social Policy in a Cold Climate' (SPCC) research programme, between 2007/8 and 2012/13, the proportion of those who were of working age and unemployed from BAME communities increased at a faster rate than white majority communities. *This shows that BAME groups have experienced a decline in employment rates and this is a clear negative impact in terms of employment inequality for these groups.* It would appear from this evidence that White communities (82% at the last Census, 2011) *are not experiencing the same negative impact and so BAME groups could said to be disproportionately negatively affected by employment inequalities.*

A study by the Institute for Social and Economic Research at the University of Essex, found British ethnic minority graduates were between 5% and 15% less likely to be employed than their white British peers six months after graduation. *This is clear evidence of a negative impact in relation to employment for BAME groups. This disparity between the success of Whites compared to the lack of success for BAME groups could result in long term unemployment, reduced opportunities to begin earning and saving into a pension or buying a property. In the long term this will cause income inequality and health inequalities as there is a clear link between low income and poor health.*

According to a 2015 report in The Guardian, the number of young people from ethnic minority backgrounds who have been unemployed for more than a year has risen by almost 50% since 2010, according to figures released by the Labour party. There are now 41,000 16- to 24-year-olds from the BAME communities who are long-term unemployed – a 49% rise from 2010, according to an analysis of official figures by the House of Commons Library. At the same time, there was a fall of 1% in overall long-term youth unemployment and a 2% fall among young white people. *This shows that BAME groups face long term unemployment which could result in persistent generational poverty. This data reveals that unemployment rates for BAME groups is on the rise which is important as it will cause mental and physical health issues for many people. Considering that many BAME live in ethnic communities there will be an impact on these communities as areas with a high proportion of long term unemployed people tend to have higher rates of crime and violence.*

Only 10% of British Somali women are in work. Only 10% of Black African women are in intermediate occupations (e.g. paramedics, police officers, and bank staff) compared to 20% of white British women, and they are under-represented at higher occupational levels too. For the BAME people who have been successful in staying in employment, their opportunities to progress to senior management positions are limited, according to the Race Disparity Audit's Ethnicity Facts and Figures report of 2016. *This is significant because if BAME groups are unable to climb a career ladder it will mean that their earning potential will be limited.* However, ethnic minorities are under-represented at senior levels and this is further reflected by recent findings from think-tank Green Park and Operation Black Vote (OBV), which showed only 4% of council authority leaders are from ethnic minority backgrounds. *This is important as not having adequate political or community representation that reflects BAME groups in their communities will result in an erosion of public trust and feelings of isolation which are undeniably negative in impact.*

Evaluation

Therefore, it would be fair to evaluate that low income disproportionally affects BAME groups. The result of this is the perpetuation of the cycle of poverty and the continuation of BAME groups facing a lack of socio-economic opportunities and inadequate representation in communities and in senior management positions. One could argue that when compared with another example of social inequality facing BAME groups, such as poor health, low income is in fact more significant because of its negative and far-reaching impact on lifestyle and attitudes about the future.

The responsibility for healthcare and welfare in the UK (Collectivist v Individualistic debate)

Argument 1 (Collectivist): Health care and welfare should be the responsibility of the government

In 2016 the UK Government under David Cameron helped to kick-start savings with a £1,200 bonus for up to 3.5 million people through new the Help to Save scheme. In addition, a £14 million investment was introduced to help turn around the lives of 25,000 struggling teens through national mentoring campaign. Moreover, almost half a million young people received a pay rise of up to £450 a year thanks to the largest increases in the National Minimum Wage for 8 years. These policies can be considered to be examples of positive government action that aimed to reduce the income gap in the UK. *Without government intervention like this it could be argued that income inequality would only increase resulting in persistent generational poverty.*

The Westminster Government claims that its aim is to support people on Universal Credit by increasing their earnings and ultimately move off benefits altogether. In order to support people on low incomes the current Conservative Government has introduced the National Living Wage - which is set to reach over £9 an hour by 2020. Introducing the National Living Wage will help to reduce the gap between rich and poor and seek to ensure a 'levelling' of society so that the UK will not be so unequal. *However, Individualists would counter this by arguing that the National Living Wage is not reflective of the real cost of living and so does not reduce social inequalities.*

The UK Government also increased the personal tax allowance to £11,850 from April 2018. This means that the amount a person can earn without being taxed has increased. This means that people should have more 'take home' pay as a result which could go far to reducing income inequalities. *It is clear that without such government intervention income inequalities may only increase.*

Therefore this policy should help the most in need. Collectivists would argue that it is the government's responsibility to tackle this inequality through the continuation of the welfare state.

Free early years provision has doubled under the current UK Government to 30 hours per week for working parents of 3 and 4 year olds. *This is significant as it shows that the government has created a strategy to get people back into work which will improve earning potential, ability to save and encourage a greater sense of purpose and self-esteem in people.*

Health inequalities are currently estimated to cost the NHS a total of at least £20 billion each year. Using taxes the UK Government funds the NHS so that is free for all at the point of access. The free NHS Health Check programme was established to reduce health inequalities by, among other strategies, reducing premature preventable death by assessing the risk of developing a condition and providing necessary treatment if a condition presents itself. This means that as a result of this free healthcare service many diseases can be diagnosed and treated which can in turn improve quality of life and increase life expectancy among the affected. *Without this government provision it is difficult to conceive how healthcare could be provided without a cost and resultant health inequalities for those that could not afford to pay for healthcare. This would mean that the rich would live and the poor would die prematurely.*

To ensure everyone enjoys the right to health, the health care provision offered by the NHS must be available, accessible, acceptable, appropriate and of equal quality irrespective of geographical location. It has been argued that it is the responsibility of the government to ensure that welfare rights are guaranteed to all citizens to reduce income, health, housing, education, gender and employment inequalities. This belief derives from the idea that this is how a 'civil society' should work. Some would argue that given the size of society it is only the government that can deliver the work of the welfare state. *This is the only way to ensure equality by offering the same universal and comprehensive provision to all people. Supporters of collectivist policies claim that only government action will be capable of tackling huge social ills such as poverty, health, gender and racial inequalities.*

Argument 2 (Individualistic): Health care and welfare should not be the responsibility of the government

Despite the fact that the NHS was set up to provide comprehensive universal physical and mental health care for all there exists a postcode lottery where some drugs are available in some areas and not in others. This results in geographic inequalities which means that the government claim to meet the needs of all UK citizens. This is mainly due to funding cuts during periods of austerity. Numbers released by ministers show NHS England will face a sharp reduction of 0.6% in real terms of per head in the financial year 2018-19. *This is important in the debate because it shows that the government cannot offer the services that a true welfare state should. Individualists would argue that the NHS is not working and as so many diseases are preventable, people should look to themselves and take greater responsibility for their own healthcare.*

One disadvantage of the government providing welfare is that it takes away responsibility from the individual, the family and the community. This can create a dependency culture in which people are dis-incentivised to work as they can receive financial benefits without having to work. Individualists would argue that without personal responsibility, there is no personal independence or freedom. The state acts as a 'nanny state' patronising and controlling its citizens. *Individualists would condemn this approach as disempowering for individuals. They would argue that individual responsibility is important as it permits personal growth and allows control over one's life.*

Benefit pay-outs (including the state pension) by the Department for Work and Pensions amounted to about £171 billion in 2015/16. Total spending on benefits and tax credits totalled approximately

£217 billion in 2015/16. This is about 11.7% of GDP and about 29.2% of total public spending. This is significant as it shows that the welfare state is incredibly expensive and the cost of its maintenance is increasing. *Some individualists would argue that this money simply funds those people who are unwilling to work. Collectivists would counter this by stating that not all unemployed people are unemployed through choice: some are medically unfit for work, are carers or perhaps suffering from a downturn in employment opportunities in their geographic area.*

Individualists would also argue that the UK will not experience significant social and educational improvement until the welfare state is either abolished or reformed so that it only provides for those in the most serious and immediate need. Welfare dependency only perpetuates welfare spending. People who work hard and pay taxes that fund the welfare state may feel anger towards those who do not make any financial contribution. *This is significant because it can create a societal divide and a polarisation of people which is detrimental to society.*

Figures from the Department for Work and Pensions show that benefit fraud cost taxpayers £1.2 billion during 2012–13, up 9% on the year before. *Individualists would argue that because the welfare state is open to abuse from fraudulent claims it should be abolished. Individualists believe that money that is allocated to the provision of benefits could be spent on building better schools, hospitals, introducing a Living Wage or increasing the salaries of teachers and nurses, for example.*

Evaluation

Overall, it would be fair to evaluate that the responsibility to improve social inequality in the UK can be found in both the collectivist and individualist arguments. Social inequality is such a huge issue to tackle that it could not be completed by individual will alone. In addition, even with individual will some people are unable to lift themselves out of poverty. Some individualists would argue that the welfare state encourages a lack of application and need to be responsible. That said, collectivists would argue that the welfare state is like a life jacket to help the most in need in society and without a collective response some people would experience even greater social inequality which would be detrimental not only to the individual but society as a whole. This is because some collectivists would argue that inequality has a negative impact on everyone not just those experiencing low income, lack of success in education, discrimination based on gender/race/age, and poor health. The reason for this is that it creates an unfair society that is divided and lacks cohesion. Greater equality could result in a stronger economy and well-being for everyone in society.

The effectiveness of government responses to tackling social inequalities.

Government response 1: Benefits

Universal Credit is a means-tested benefit for people of working-age who are on a low income. It replaces six existing means-tested benefits (Income Support, Income-based Jobseeker's Allowance, Income-related Employment and Support Allowance, Housing Benefit, Child Tax Credit and Working Tax Credit). A single person under 25 would receive approximately £250 per month via UC whereas a couple (in which at least one person is over 25) would receive approximately £500 per month via UC. People that have children receive approximately £230 per month on top of their standard UC benefit payment. By 2022, more than seven million households will receive Universal Credit - at least half of which will be in work. *It could be argued that the government's introduction of UC is effective in tackling social inequality because it has provided a simplified way that those most in need can gain access to financial assistance. UC is means-tested so this means that it can be considered a fair system rather than disincentive to work.* Those on low incomes can top up their salaries with UC so that they remain in work.

However, it could be argued that there are some major limitations to UC and its effectiveness in tackling social inequality. In order to claim UC a person must be willing to take any job offered. *This means that people could feel under considerable pressure to take a job that they do not want and this could have a negative impact on their mental health as they may feel very unhappy, unfulfilled and disempowered.* Claimants also have to accept that they may have to work unpaid for 6 months as part of the 'Workfare' scheme. This can result in some firms exploiting the 'free labour' made available to them. A report in The Mirror found that job seekers involved in the Workfare scheme are no more likely to get a job at the end of their unpaid work than those who refused to take part. Only 25% of people that completed the Workfare programme managed to gain employment after the period of unpaid work. This lack of income can result in many people turning to 'loan sharks' or payday loans in order to gain access to the funds that they need to live and support their families. There is also a benefit cap with UC. The Benefit Cap is a limit to the total amount of money a person can receive from benefits. A person's benefits will be reduced if they get more than the limit that applies for their circumstances - this means they will get less Housing Benefit or Universal Credit. This may have a negative impact on larger families or those living in expensive areas of London where rents are higher. There have been a number of case in which UC claimants have had to move out of their social accommodation in expensive London boroughs due to the cap on payments. This means that some areas of the country, notably London, will only house the wealthy and homes may lie vacant as they have been purchased by wealthy foreign nationals who will not live in these second homes for significant periods of time. *This could create even more social inequality rather than reduce it.* This cap on housing benefit may force people to move to poorer areas, creating what has become known as low-income 'ghettos'. A 2016 Department for Work and Pensions (DWP) report found that one in four claimants have waited longer than six weeks for the administrative processing of UC claims. This has been a significant factor in pushing some claimants into rent arrears. *This only serves to exacerbate low income as a social inequality.*

A person born on or before 5 November 1953 could get between £100 and £300 to help pay for their heating bills. Figures from the Department of Energy & Climate Change show that 2.4 million households live in fuel poverty – almost 11% of all English households. Households are regarded as being in fuel poverty if they need to spend more than 10% of their income to heat their home to an adequate standard. In England this is defined as 21C in the living room and 18C in other occupied rooms. This is known as a 'Winter Fuel Payment' (WFP). Eligible people usually get a Winter Fuel Payment automatically if get the State Pension or another social security benefit (not Housing Benefit, Council Tax Reduction, Child Benefit or Universal Credit). About 12.26 million people received the tax-free allowance in 2015-6, at a total cost of just over £2bn. *This could be regarded as an effective way to tackle fuel poverty in the UK.* The approximate payment made each December is between £100 and £300 per month depending on age and whether the claimant lives alone or not. This could help some of the most vulnerable individuals in society especially those whose only 'income' is a state pension. *This benefit can help to heat people's homes and mitigate the negative health effects of the cold weather, notably pneumonia.* According the Office of National Statistics (ONS) the number of 'excess winter deaths' (the increase in the death rate across the population that occurs each winter) in England and Wales during 2011-12 was around 24,000 with the highest mortality rate seen in January. The ONS have calculated that between 1950-51 and 2011-12, there have been around 2,663,390 excess winter deaths in the UK. Females aged 85 and over experience the greatest number of excess winter deaths. This is because a higher proportion of the female population are aged 75 and over. In 2013 The Strategic Society Centre reported that a large proportion of excess winter deaths are attributable to respiratory problems or cardiovascular diseases, not least because being cold can lower a person's heart rate and increase blood pressure. The impact of the winter fuel payments have been largely positive and have helped to save the most vulnerable lives. Responsibility for the WFP was devolved to the Scottish Parliament under the Scotland Act 2016. The SNP pledged to protect the WFP in 2015 and in 2017, also to extend eligibility to families with severely disabled children. The SNP have shown a commitment to helping pensioners, many of whom have contributed to the state throughout their lives. The SNP have also shown benevolence to the most vulnerable families by helping to fund increasing fuel costs. In 2017 Npower increased its electricity prices by 15% and Scottish Power increased its standard domestic gas and electricity prices by an average of £86 from 31 March 2017. These energy price hikes will impact people on low incomes or benefits and as such the WFP is an effective government response to tackle social inequalities in the UK, particularly in relation to health and income inequality. Four million (15%) of households in the UK are not connected to the mains gas grid and people in this situation generally have very little choice in their source of heating fuel. Households with oil-fired central heating, and those using solid fuel or liquid petroleum gas

(LPG) to heat their homes, are much more likely to be in fuel poverty than "on-grid" households. *This is significant because many people that could benefit from the WFP are unable to do so.* This is because the people that use off-grid energy sources have to pre-pay for their fuel and if they have to wait until December to receive the payment when fuel costs are at their highest. *This means that for some people the WFP does not effectively tackle the inequalities that they face.*

The 2017 Conservative manifesto set out plans to begin means-testing the winter fuel payment. Labour claims that up to 10 million pensioners are set to lose the benefit under the Conservative Government's plans. Theresa May claimed that the money saved would help bridge the £2.8bn social care funding gap. The Conservative manifesto in Scotland says the winter fuel allowance will not be means-tested. *Means-testing a benefit will ensure that the most in need will receive financial assistance and this could mean that the WFP will help the most vulnerable pensioners. A counter argument to the practice of means-testing benefits is that universal benefits are much more simple and efficient to administer.* Means testing requires a huge amount of bureaucracy which will be costly and eat up funds that could be redirected to those who could be claimants of the WFP. It is probable that the people that could claim non-means-tested WFP have already paid for them in their taxes paid over their life time. Means-testing benefits is considered by some to be unfair as the Government is denying people the entitlements that they have contributed to.

Government response 2: Housing Provision

The UK government is currently helping local councils and developers work with local communities to plan and build better homes for everyone. This includes building affordable housing, improving the quality of rented housing, helping more people to buy a home, and providing housing support for vulnerable people. In June 2018 the UK Government announced a ten year funding deal worth £22.4 million. This Fund will accelerate the delivery of 1,300 new homes at Wing in Cambridge. The first phase of the development will comprise of 350 private homes and 150 affordable homes – including shared ownership and affordable rent tenures. *This is an example of how effectively the Westminster government is in tackling housing inequality.* One of the biggest problems facing the government is that there are simply not enough affordable homes for people to rent or buy. As a result, more people apply to be placed on a waiting list for social housing. This wait can force many vulnerable people into unsuitable housing or even into homelessness. By helping to fund housing development, the UK government is taking positive and effective action to tackle housing inequality.

The Scottish Government is currently committed to increasing the amount of council housing and protecting social housing for the future by ending the 'Right to Buy' scheme. The 'Right to Buy' scheme (which gives tenants the right to buy their rented home at a discounted price) ended for council and housing association tenants in Scotland on 31 July 2016. The Scottish Federation of Housing Associations (SFHA) Chief Executive stated that this was a step forward in terms of supplying "truly affordable homes to people on low incomes". Kevin Stewart, SNP MSP and Housing Minister said that "with thousands of people on waiting lists for council and housing association houses, it was only right for us to scrap this scheme as we could no longer afford to see the social sector lose out on badly needed homes". He also stated the SNP's commitment to build 50,000 affordable homes over the lifetime of the current parliament, including 35,000 social homes. This is significant as it shows an effective Scottish Government response to tackling housing in equality in Scotland as ending 'Right to Buy' will prevent the sale of 15,500 homes over a 10-year period. *It will protect the existing stock of social rented homes, and ensure social landlords can help people who need social housing and could help to tackle housing inequalities.*

There are more than 1.8 million households in England waiting for a social home – an increase of 81% since 1997, according to the housing and homelessness charity, Shelter. Shelter also reported that two thirds of households on the waiting list have been waiting for more than a year and nearly 41,000 households with dependent children were living in temporary accommodation at the end of December 2012. *This is significant because the government has not been effective in providing enough social housing for the most vulnerable people in society. This means that these people may face a chaotic and dangerous lifestyle while living on the streets.*

The Bedroom Tax was introduced by the UK government in 2012 with the aim of reducing benefits for people living in council or housing association homes who are considered to have a spare bedroom. A person whose home has more bedrooms than they need will experience a percentage reduction to their eligible rent. 14% will be taken off if they have one extra bedroom, or 25% will be taken off if you they two extra bedrooms. This means that many people will fall into rent arrears and may risk making themselves 'intentionally homeless'. This would mean that their local council is not obliged to offer them alternative accommodation. This would result in a person or family facing a vulnerable situation and certain income and housing inequality.

In 2014 the Scottish Parliament voted to reject Westminster's bedroom tax and plans were made to mitigate the tax. Finance Secretary, John Swinney said the Scottish Government would spend more than £244million helping those affected by UK Government welfare cuts between 2013-14 and 2015-16 – at the expense of spending in other areas. He committed £15million so the entire £50million required would be available in benefits to social housing tenants judged to have a spare bedroom. *This shows that the Scottish Government have taken effective action to help people in Scotland impacted by the Bedroom Tax. This means that people who would have had to pay an extra tax for 'under occupancy' in their homes no longer have to face an additional financial pressure or face taking in a lodger to make up the tax payment.*

Government Response 3: Education Provision

The Fair Education Alliance (a coalition of education organisations, charities and businesses established to build a fairer education for all by 2022) reported in 2017 that key measures needed to be adopted by the Government to narrow the attainment gap at all levels of education. Similarly the Joseph Rowntree Foundation (JRF) found that the attainment gap between pupils from the richest and poorest backgrounds in Scotland is wider than in many similar countries with a clear literacy gap in Primary 4 that widens by Primary 7. The Scottish Survey of Literacy and Numeracy found in 2016 an attainment gap of 14–17% for reading, 21% for writing, and 12-28% for numeracy from primary through to secondary school.

The Scottish Government introduced the Scottish Attainment Challenge in 2015 with the aim of achieving equity in education. It is underpinned by The National Improvement Framework, Curriculum for Excellence and Getting it Right for Every Child. (GIRFEC). The focus of this initiative is to improve literacy, numeracy and health and well-being among young people in Scotland. £750million was committed to this programme that is focused on areas with the highest concentration of social and economic deprivation in Scotland. The 'Challenge Authorities' as they are known, are Glasgow, Dundee, Inverclyde, West Dunbartonshire, North Ayrshire, Clackmannanshire, North Lanarkshire, East Ayrshire and Renfrewshire. *This is significant as it shows a clear commitment from the Scottish Government to tackle directly education inequality in Scotland.* The funding was committed initially to primary schools in order to give Scotland's youngest learners the best grounding for educational attainment. An Interim Report published in 2017 found that The Attainment Scotland Fund was found to be a driver for change and cohesion. *As a result of the fund, there was an increased awareness, understanding and shared commitment to address the impact of poverty on attainment across local authorities and schools.* In March 2018 the Scottish Government published an evaluation of its programmes to narrow the attainment gap. It found that 78% of surveyed head teachers saw improvements in tackling the attainment gap in literacy, numeracy and health and wellbeing as a result of the fund. *This shows that the initiative has had a positive impact on attitudes towards decreasing the attainment gap however the poverty related attainment gap continues to exist. This means that while progress has been made and a commitment to narrowing the attainment gap has been made, the underlying root cause of education inequality – low income – has not been tackled fully and therefore the impact of the Attainment Fund is limited.*

In 2016, the gap in university entry between children from low-income families and their more affluent peers increased fractionally; this was the first increase in the gap since 2010. Children from more affluent backgrounds are currently just over twice as likely to enter university as those from low-income families; this has reduced from almost three times as likely in 2006. The SNP have tried to narrow the gap in university entry by offering free university tuition fees for Scottish (and EU) students attending Scottish universities. Former First Minister Alex Salmond said the "rocks would melt in the sun" before he would contemplate introducing tuition fees. A completed degree in Dentistry/Medicine or Veterinary Medicine at Glasgow University will cost £46,250 (2018/19 entry) for a student from England, Wales or Northern Ireland. A Scottish student will not have to pay these fees and will attend without charge (Accommodation/books are not included although extra funding is available from The Student Awards Agency for Scotland (SAAS) which provides living cost grants. These may be granted if a a person has an adult dependent they care for, or are a lone parent. If a person is eligible they can receive up to £2,640. There is also help for those leaving care). At English and Northern Irish universities, a Scottish and EU student can be charged up to £9,250 per year for tuition. SNP education ministers have argued that free tuition means a university education is "based on the ability to learn, not the ability to pay". *This policy could go far in balancing educational attainment levels among the country's richest and poorest. This could impact positively income levels for those able to attend university as those with degrees are statistically more likely to earn more over their lifetime that those without a degree.*

A report in The Herald (2015) stated that academics from Edinburgh University said there was no evidence free tuition had increased access to higher education for pupils from the poorest backgrounds. They concluded that public investment would be better targeted at raising attainment in schools in the most deprived areas of Scotland - with a graduate tax one way of raising additional funds for the university sector. This is significant as it shows that this free tuition strategy has been criticised for over-prioritising university education over funding for schools and colleges. Critics argue that spending a greater proportion of money on schools and colleges in the most deprived areas of Scotland would have the most impact on reducing education inequalities. Without a solid education foundation at a younger age, many pupils will not achieve the grades required for university entry. The Sutton Trust's Access in Scotland Study (2016) found that children from the most deprived areas are four times less likely to go to university than those from the wealthiest areas. An article in The Telegraph (2015) reported that official statistics obtained under the Freedom of Information (FOI) Act found that the number of Scots accepted at Glasgow, Edinburgh, Aberdeen and Dundee universities has fallen over the past two years, but over the same period the number of applicants from other EU countries given a place has increased. The FOI figures showed the proportion of Scottish undergraduates at Glasgow University fell from 72% (11,268) in 2011/12 to 63% in 2013/14 (10,656). Over the same period the proportion of EU students increased by three percentage points to 14.4%, from 1,805 to 2,437. *This is significant as it shows that while 'free degrees' may be on offer, the number of places are restricted for Scottish students.* The SNP Government have stated that the number of places for Scottish students at Scottish universities has been capped. *This shows that this initiative may not have been entirely effective in reducing education inequalities.*

Government Response 4: Healthcare Provision

The Scottish Government has stated that it is committed to reducing inequalities in health in order to make Scotland a better, healthier place for everyone, no matter where they live. Good Places, Better Health (GPBH) was launched in 2008 as the Scottish Government's strategy on health and the environment. One of the aims of this initiative was to tackle childhood obesity by encouraging breastfeeding, limiting children's access to unhealthy snacks by removing vending machines from public buildings and banning fast food vans from outside schools. The provision of school-based physical activities have also been increased. *This is effective as the Scottish government has made a clear link between obesity, diet and exercise. By tackling this issue the government has aimed to create positive habits of healthy eating and physical activity. This will improve the overall quality of people's lives and reduce the strain on health services.* In 2015, 65% of adults aged 16 and over were overweight, including 29% that were obese. Levels of obesity increased between 1995 and 2008, but have remained relatively stable since then. *This shows that the introduction of GPBH in 2008 may have had a direct impact on stabilising obesity levels in Scotland and therefore this government action could be regarded as effective.* However, 15% of children in Scotland in 2016 were considered obese. Given that obesity is the UK's second largest single preventable cause of cancer after smoking, it is clear that GPBH has not been entirely successful. *Environmental and social factors can be drivers of obesity in both children and adults and so it would be unfair to overly criticise this government policy.*

In March 2016 the Chancellor of the Exchequer, George Osborne, announced the introduction (in April 2018) of a new 'sugar tax' aimed at high-sugar drinks. This tax reaches up to 24p per litre depending on sugar content. A typical can of fizzy juice can contain up to nine teaspoons of sugar. Scottish households spend more than any other UK nation on soft drinks, at £2.60 per week compared to the British average of £1.90 per week. The UK Government have stated that this money will be used to combat childhood obesity and fund sports programmes in primary schools. This could be considered an effective strategy to tackle excessive sugar consumption which can cause obesity. *The sugar tax has been criticised because this type of tax will hit the poorest hardest as statistically this group tends to spend a greater proportion of their income on 'sin taxes' and VAT.* The Office for National Statistics (ONS) found that the poorest fifth spent 9.8% of their disposable income on goods attracting VAT in 2009/10, while the richest fifth spent 5.3%. The Institute for Economic Affairs found that the poorest 20% of Britons spends 37% of their disposable income on 'sin taxes' which, from April 2018 includes the 'sugar tax'. *Therefore it would be fair to assess the 'sugar tax' as being effective in terms of health inequalities, however it may be ineffective as it will exacerbate income inequalities among the poorest of society who tend to purchase more sugary drinks.*

According to a 2016 Scottish Government report, 17% more alcohol was sold per adult in Scotland than in England & Wales. In Scotland, on average, there are 24 deaths a week that are alcohol-related, and death rates are 1.5 times the level recorded in 1980. In May 2018 the Scottish Government introduced a minimum price of 50p per unit of alcohol. *This could be considered an effective government response to tackling health inequalities as researchers from Sheffield University found that a minimum unit price of 50 pence is estimated to result in 121 fewer deaths per annum by year 20 of the policy; and a fall in hospital admissions of just over 2,000 per annum by year 20 of the policy.* However a loophole has been found as Scots can order alcohol online from England to avoid the higher priced alcohol. *Therefore this strategy is limited in its effectiveness to tackle health inequalities.* Research undertaken in 2013 by the Institute of Economic Affairs found that alcohol taxes consume 2 to 4% of the income of moderate drinkers in the bottom fifth of households. People on low incomes that consume alcohol are more likely to purchase cheaper alcohol brands. The minimum pricing of alcohol will impact directly this socio-economic group. This policy could be considered ineffective as research has shown that alcohol consumption actually rises with income. The Institute of Alcohol Studies found that in 2011 29% of adults with high earnings drank heavily (exceeding 8 units) on at least one day in the week whereas for adults with lower earnings this was much lower at 20%. *Therefore the minimum pricing strategy is limited in its effectiveness as it targets those on low incomes when evidence shows that those earning higher incomes have a higher propensity to drink alcohol and be harmed by its negative health impact.*

The Smoking Ban came into force in Scotland in March 2006. Scotland was the first country in the UK to ban smoking in public places. The rationale behind this government policy was to protect people from the effects of second-hand smoke. *This was an effective government response as it prioritised people's health and aimed to reduce health inequalities in Scotland. It was also effective as it changed social norms around smoking around others and in enclosed spaces.* The pressure group Ash Scotland found that the Smoking ban also resulted in a reduction in the rate of child asthma admissions of 18% per year compared to an increase of 5% per year in the years preceding it. *This shows that this was an effective government policy and did reduce health inequalities. The Scottish Government has reported that the ban may have also helped to reduce the number of teenagers taking up smoking by a fifth and an 86% reduction in second-hand smoke in bars. This is significant as it shows how effective this ban has been in terms of improving the health of Scottish people.* The Scottish Government followed up the Smoking ban with a banning of the display of tobacco products in shops and making it illegal to smoke in cars when children are present. *This can be regarded as an effective government response as it has helped to safeguard the respiratory health of children and reduced the rates of heart disease in Scotland by 17%.*

Evaluation

Overall it would be fair to evaluate that government responses have been integral to tackling social inequalities. The most effective strategies have been the introduction of the Smoking ban and the widening of opportunity for Scottish students to attend universities without paying fees. Tackling social inequalities in relation to health, income, education and housing is a fundamental social, economic and political challenge which is costly and complex for any government. It is difficult to see how the UK Government intends to prioritise the reduction of social inequalities when we consider the £12bn of welfare spending cuts made by the Conservative Government. The aim behind these cuts to public spending is to combat economic austerity. Critics would argue that these spending cuts impact negatively the most vulnerable in society, notably the disabled and those on low incomes. As a result of government spending cuts some families have been forced to rely on food banks, relocate against their will, take unpaid work, turn to high interest unsecured loans and experience humiliating health care 'tests' to ascertain the extent of their disability and inability to work. One might argue that these spending cuts have only served to exacerbate inequality and increase the gap between rich and poor. The Scottish Government have committed to helping the most vulnerable in society however this is difficult to achieve as a devolved power when funding for benefits is derived mainly from Westminster. However in 2016 the Scottish Parliament's devolved powers were extended to allow it to make new benefits, top-up and change the frequency of the payment of UK wide benefits such as Universal Credit, Tax Credits and Child Benefit among others. If the Scottish Government is able to design its own social security system that best meets the needs of the Scottish people it may be that the result will be a more effective response to tackling income, health, education and housing inequalities in Scotland.

Glossary

Absolute poverty The level of poverty defined in terms of the minimum requirements for basic subsistence (food, shelter, clothing).

Affluent Rich, wealthy.

Attainment gap The gap between the education achievements of affluent pupils compared with pupils from socially deprived areas. It has been found that 15 year-olds from poorer families in Scotland were found to be roughly 2-3 years behind their better-off peers in recent research comparing performance in science, maths and reading.

Boroughs A town, or a district within a large town, which has its own council.

Breadwinner The breadwinner in a family is the person in it who earns the money that the family needs for essential things.

Cardiovascular Relating to the heart and blood vessels. Often associated with cardiovascular or heart disease.

Carer's Allowance A Government financial benefit for people who spend at least 35 hours a week providing regular care to someone who has a disability.

Census An official survey of the population of a country that is carried out in order to find out how many people live there and to obtain details of such things as people's ages and jobs.

Chronic Severe.

Cohesion Fits well, united.

Collectivism The political belief that a country's industries and services should be owned and controlled by the state or by all the people in a country. Socialism and communism are both forms of collectivism.

Convenience foods Fast food or food that is quick and easy to prepare.

Correlation A connection or link.

Counterparts A person or thing identical to or closely resembling another.

Debilitating Weakening, tiring, exhausting, draining.

Diabetes A medical condition in which someone has too much sugar in their blood.

Discrimination The practice of treating one person or group of people less fairly or less well than other people or groups.

Disempower To deprive (a person) of power or authority.

Disparity Inequality, difference, dissimilarity.

Disproportionate Out of proportion; unequal.

Diverse Varied, diversified, dissimilar.

Earning potential The highest possible income a person could be paid. The term is also often used to identify the amount of money that an individual can earn throughout his or her years in employment.

Entitlements Something to which a person is entitled; specifically benefits provided to qualifying persons under certain government programmes, such as Carer's Allowance.

Equitable Something that is equitable is fair and reasonable in a way that gives equal treatment to everyone.

Equivalent Equal or interchangeable in value, quantity, significance etc.

EU The European Union is an organisation of European countries which have joint policies on matters such as trade, agriculture, and finance.

Exploit To take advantage of (a person, situation, etc.), especially unethically or unjustly for one's own ends.

Foreign nationals A person residing in a country without the right to permanent residence in that country

Gender segregation The separation of people according to their gender

Generational poverty A family having lived in poverty for at least two generations.

Glasgow Effect The unexplained poor health and low life expectancy of residents of Glasgow, Scotland, compared to the rest of the United Kingdom and Europe.

Income The money that someone earns

Individualism The belief that economics and politics should not be controlled by the state.

Initiative First step or the power to introduce new laws.

Intentionally homeless Local councils will assess the reasons that someone has become homeless. If someone is found to have become homeless because they left accommodation that they could have stayed in. The council could decide a person has made themselves intentionally homeless if they lose their home because of something that they deliberately did or failed to do.

Life expectancy A statistical measure of the average time a person is expected to live, based on the year of their birth, current age and other demographic factors including gender and geographical location.

Life-limiting These are life-threatening conditions where there is no reasonable hope of cure; and from which children or young people will die before reaching adulthood. Some of these conditions cause progressive deterioration.

Lifestyle choices These are the decisions people make about the things that they do in their life such as exercise, smoke, drink alcohol, take drugs, eat health foods or otherwise.

Living Wage The minimum income necessary for a worker to meet their needs that are considered to be basic. The Living Wage is set independently by the Living Wage Foundation and is calculated according to the basic cost of living in the UK. Employers choose to pay the Living Wage on a voluntary basis. The Living Wage is therefore different to the National Living Wage currently set and administered by the Westminster Government. The Living Wage mustn't be mixed up with the government's National Living Wage. This should not be confused with the National Living Wage. The Living Wage is an advisory figure offered by the Living Wage Foundation. It is not enforceable by law.

Loan shark A person or group that offer loans at extremely high interest rates. The term usually refers to illegal activity, but may also refer to aggressive lending with extremely high interest rates Loan sharks sometimes use blackmail or threats of violence to ensure repayment.

Lodger A person who rents accommodation in another person's house.

Lone parent A parent who is not married and does not have a partner, who is bringing up a child or children by themselves.

Manifesto A public declaration of policy and aims, especially one issued before an election by a political party or candidate.

Marginally To only a limited extent; slightly.

Means-tested A determination of whether an individual or family is eligible for government assistance, based upon whether the individual or family has enough money to do without that financial assistance.

Mortality rate Also known as death rate. A mortality rate is the number of deaths during a particular period of time among a particular type or group of people Mortality rate is expressed in units of deaths per 1,000 individuals per year.

Nanny state A derogatory term for a government that makes decisions for people that they might otherwise make for themselves. A nanny state tries to protect its citizens too much and makes them rely on the state too much.

National Living Wage The government's National Living Wage became law on 1 April 2016 under ex-Tory Chancellor George Osborne and is the lowest rate that can be paid to employees 25-years-old and over. The National Living Wage is the amount of money all employees aged over 25 are legally entitled to. It used to be known as the National Minimum Wage, but it was re-branded in 2016. The National Living Wage increased from £7.50 to £7.83 for those aged 25 and over. The 33 pence-an-hour rise was introduced on Sunday April 1, 2018. The compulsory National Living Wage was introduced in 2016.

National Minimum Wage The National Minimum Wage is the amount which workers aged under 25, but of school-leaving age, are entitled to. However, the amount differs depending on age and whether the worker is on an apprenticeship scheme. Workers aged 21-24 were paid £7.05 - and it went up to £7.38 from April 1, 2018. The wage increased from £5.60 to £5.90 for 18 to 20-year-olds, and from £4.05 to £4.20 for under 18s. However, apprentices were only entitled to £3.50 if they are under-19 - this increased to £3.70 from April 1, 2018. In April 2018, the minimum wage for 25-year-olds rose from £7.50 to £7.83 an hour. The national limits are legally binding. It is a criminal offence for employers to not pay someone the National Minimum Wage or National Living Wage. The National Minimum Wage is used interchangeably with the term National Living Wage.

Obesity The term "obese" describes a person who's very overweight, with a lot of body fat. The NHS state that if a person has a BMI of 30 to 39.9 it means that they are obese while a score of 40 or above means that a person is severely obese.

OECD The Organisation for Economic Co-operation and Development is an intergovernmental economic organisation with 37 member countries, founded in 1961 to stimulate economic progress and world trade.

Payday loans A relatively small amount of money lent at a high rate of interest on the agreement that it will be repaid when the borrower receives their next wages.

Polarisation A sharp division, as of a population or group, into opposing factions.

Perpetuate To make (something) continue indefinitely.

Preceding Coming before something in order, position, or time.

Premature Occurring or done before the usual or proper time; too early.

Recession A period of reduced economic activity.

Relative poverty The condition in which people lack the minimum amount of income needed in order to maintain the average standard of living in the society in which they live.

Respiratory Relating to or affecting respiration or the organs of respiration

Russell Group universities A group of 24 top public research universities in the UK. Members of this group include Oxford and Cambridge universities, Glasgow University and Edinburgh University.

Salary A fixed amount of money that a person is paid for the work that they do.

Sedentary lifestyle A life that does not include exercise or other physical activity.

Sin taxes A tax on certain goods thought to be harmful to society, such as alcohol, soft drinks and fast foods.

Social gradient A term used to show the difference between people who have low income, lack of success in education and poor health and those who are more advantaged.

Social housing Homes that are affordable for people on low incomes and/or benefits. This accommodation is provided by councils.

Social ills Also referred to as 'social problems'. These are issues in a society that are undesirable for some people in the community. Examples include crime and racism.

Social mobility The movement of individuals or families between social grades or classes. It denotes a change in social status in terms of education level, employment status, income level, location, type or ownership of home, etc.

Societal divide The gap between groups in society. This gap could be based on income, class, gender, ethnicity, religious faith, political viewpoints, etc.

Status anxiety The worry individuals can experience about their place in society, perhaps in terms of their employment status or income. It relates to the fear about the way people perceive each other and whether they are as good as or better than others.

Universal Credit (UC) A payment to help with living costs. It is paid monthly - or twice a month for some people in Scotland. People are eligible if they are on a low income or out of work.

Value Added Tax (VAT) This is an amount of money added to goods and services. In the UK it is currently 20% of the value of the price of the goods or services.

Vulnerable Exposed to the threat of being harmed.

Welfare state A government that plays a central role in protecting and promoting the social and economic well-being of its citizens. A welfare state can provide healthcare, education, benefits and housing for citizens in need. Liberal politician, William Beveridge proposed setting up a welfare state in the UK in the early 1940s. He advised that there were 'Five Giants' (poverty, disease, ignorance, squalor and idleness) that needed to be defeated to create a 'better' Britain. The post-war Labour government aimed to make Beveridge's vision a reality by creating the NHS, providing free education, social housing and full employment.

Worklessness Having no paid work or employment.

About the author

Hannah Young has been a Modern Studies teacher in Scotland for 15 years and is an experienced SQA marker.

Printed by Amazon Italia Logistica S.r.l.
Torrazza Piemonte (TO), Italy